NO BAD DAYS

WHEN YOU HAVE WHEELS, FRIENDS AND MUSIC

MAUREEN ASPINWALL

Grosvenor House
Publishing Limited

This book is published by
Grosvenor House Publishing Ltd
Link House
140 The Broadway, Tolworth, Surrey, KT6 7HT.
www.grosvenorhousepublishing.co.uk

A CIP record for this book
is available from the British Library

ISBN 978-1-80381-918-1
eBook ISBN 978-1-80381-919-8

All proceeds from the sale of this book will go to the charity
Choose Love https:// chooselove.org/

CHOOSE
LOVE

"We are pioneering a new movement in humanitarian aid: fast, flexible and transparent. We go where the need is greatest, find the local organisations doing the most effective work, and give them what they need to help people – whether that's funding, material aid or volunteers. With this model, we've managed to reach over 4.8 million people through over 476 projects in 41 countries, with 82% of your donations going directly towards supporting refugees."

For Rita and John

This is an account of the fun and games I had over a two-year period following the band BΔSTILLE, written primarily for fans of the band.

I have included over twenty familiar song titles, some hidden, some not, and a few favourite lyrics for genuine fans to find.

My descriptions of the band are mostly my own opinions and hopefully some true facts.
Any mistakes are unintentional.

'Been there, done that, bought the t-shirt'

NO BAD DAYS
WHEN YOU HAVE WHEELS, FRIENDS AND MUSIC

1. Not so close encounters

I was diagnosed with primary progressive multiple sclerosis twelve years ago and was sent on my way without any treatment available. For me it seems to be one of the least debilitating versions of MS with the effects appearing extremely slowly. Currently I only have disobedient legs, difficulty balancing and talking. Most of the rest of me works perfectly well. At concerts, shows and events I use a variety of contraptions to get around.

 My full name is Maureen, but all my special friends and family call me **Mo**. I have lived in Berkshire, UK for many, many years with my husband **John**, and we have three grown-up children and five grandchildren.

I have grey hair, wear glasses and I'm round and cuddlesome. I love most kinds of music and really enjoy going to concerts with friends who help and look after me. John could go with me, but he likes a different kind of music and I prefer artists who are younger than me. 😏

I quickly realised when retirement came that quilting and gardening were not particularly exciting hobbies, but then the Covid lockdown began and it seemed as though we were living in a world gone mad. It was lucky that I had something I could do while hiding away. At this time everyone was told to stay indoors while the disease spread around the world. Several performers were doing little shows from their living rooms and anyone could watch them online. Of course, the singers were on their own too, without their bands and shut indoors.

My favourite was **Dan Smith**, the lead singer from Bastille, who can sing and play the piano very well. I confess that I freaked out when it looked as though Dan was playing a left-handed piano! Low notes on the right! It was a few ~~minutes~~ hours before I understood! He also ran a book club and a 'foreign' film club. These distraction tactics were designed to take us away from the life outside and they were great fun, especially the jingles written to hint at the country the films came from. Interviews with producers and actors involved in the films added to the diversion.

When Covid isolation rules were eventually withdrawn, we were told that we could, if we wished, get close to each other again. The relief seemed to manifest itself in excessive hugging between family, friends and sometimes complete strangers, because we could. An enjoyable new phenomenon to me!

Dan announced that Bastille would be playing at a festival. I told my daughter **Kate** about it and she said "Ooh, are we going?" and I said, "I'd love to, how about you?" and Kate replied "Abso-blooming-lutely!" That's how we talk in our family!

The festival was huge and the wheelchair platform was a long way from the stage, with about 40,000 fans between us and the performers, but we could hear it all and still had a good time. Initially I wondered why there were so many children on the stage but they turned out to be adults! Bastille performed a short set, surprising many fans with re-orchestrated versions of their songs.

My favourite was **Dan Smith**, the lead singer from Bastille, who can sing and play the piano very well. I confess that I freaked out when it looked as though Dan was playing a left-handed piano! Low notes on the right! It was a few ~~minutes~~ hours before I understood! He also ran a book club and a 'foreign' film club. These distraction tactics were designed to take us away from the life outside and they were great fun, especially the jingles written to hint at the country the films came from. Interviews with producers and actors involved in the films added to the diversion.

When Covid isolation rules were eventually withdrawn, we were told that we could, if we wished, get close to each other again. The relief seemed to manifest itself in excessive hugging between family, friends and sometimes complete strangers, because we could. An enjoyable new phenomenon to me!

Dan announced that Bastille would be playing at a festival. I told my daughter **Kate** about it and she said "Ooh, are we going?" and I said, "I'd love to, how about you?" and Kate replied "Abso-blooming-lutely!" That's how we talk in our family!

The festival was huge and the wheelchair platform was a long way from the stage, with about 40,000 fans between us and the performers, but we could hear it all and still had a good time. Initially I wondered why there were so many children on the stage but they turned out to be adults! Bastille performed a short set, surprising many fans with re-orchestrated versions of their songs.

NO BAD DAYS
WHEN YOU HAVE WHEELS, FRIENDS AND MUSIC

1. Not so close encounters

I was diagnosed with primary progressive multiple sclerosis twelve years ago and was sent on my way without any treatment available. For me it seems to be one of the least debilitating versions of MS with the effects appearing extremely slowly. Currently I only have disobedient legs, difficulty balancing and talking. Most of the rest of me works perfectly well. At concerts, shows and events I use a variety of contraptions to get around.

 My full name is Maureen, but all my special friends and family call me **Mo**. I have lived in Berkshire, UK for many, many years with my husband **John**, and we have three grown-up children and five grandchildren.

I have grey hair, wear glasses and I'm round and cuddlesome. I love most kinds of music and really enjoy going to concerts with friends who help and look after me. John could go with me, but he likes a different kind of music and I prefer artists who are younger than me. 😉

I quickly realised when retirement came that quilting and gardening were not particularly exciting hobbies, but then the Covid lockdown began and it seemed as though we were living in a world gone mad. It was lucky that I had something I could do while hiding away. At this time everyone was told to stay indoors while the disease spread around the world. Several performers were doing little shows from their living rooms and anyone could watch them online. Of course, the singers were on their own too, without their bands and shut indoors.

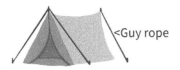<Guy rope

My mobility scooter didn't particularly like going through the grass and it was especially hard work in a crowd with people walking in front of me. My grandson William and I were dancing in the dark trying to find our way back to our campervan and I accidentally drove the scooter over a guy-rope and nearly demolished a tent! William and some passing teenagers eventually untangled me. Luckily, no-one was in the tent!

William and his Granny Mo and some cool festival headwear waiting for Bastille.

Kyle Simmons, Dan Smith, Chris 'Woody' Wood and Will Farquarson

And so the story began, and you will find it is mostly about the band Bastille.

2. Let me introduce you to the band

Googling the band and watching the ReOrchestrated documentary and performances on YouTube led to the realisation that they are all amazing humans with a vast range of accomplishments, *some* of which are mentioned below.

The band has four members *but* **Charlie Barnes,** a guitarist, is a phenomenal added extra who perpetually travels with them. Renowned for his energetic antics when on stage performing, Charlie will also sing, play drums and keyboards. Charlie was selected to be the arranger and musical director of acoustic versions of their songs and covers for the MTV Unplugged special performance. My favourite was a barn-dance version of 'Happier' with lots of brass. He is also producing a new album of his own music and has a dog called Luna.

Woody is the drummer and has been seen playing all types of percussion from slapping his thigh, advancing to a child's xylophone, tom toms, bongos, electronic drums, a huge drum kit and lately kettle drums. Woody sings backing vocals and can also play guitar. He plays football and cricket and is a superfan of Plymouth Argyle FC and is the only member of the band with long hair. Often he's the main person to get the crowd clapping and singing, conducting from his position behind the drums. Usually, his drumsticks are thrown into the audience, carefully, at the end of a show.

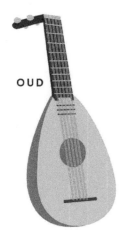

OUD

Will Farquarson, the bassist, is the oldest and most sophisticated member of the band. More of a country gent fashion-wise than a hip pop musician! Rumour has it that as a teenager he had long hair and was more of a hippie, but I have no proof of that! He can apparently play any instrument with strings, from cello to guitar, oud to piano and everything in between. Will has also acted, is an artist, can ride a horse and is able to fly a plane. He is also a backing singer and on the stage he is the complete opposite of **Charlie**.

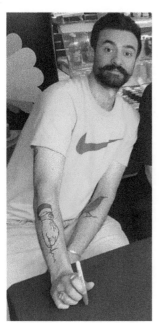

Kyle Simmons is the most stylish dresser of the group and in his own words, 'the light relief of the band!' providing the laughs. Starting with a saxophone at school, for the band he plays the keyboards, organ, drums, guitar and xylophone and is also a singer and is very fond of cats and gaming. Kyle is the original voice of Morell, a cryptozoologist, and Video Revachol, in the video game *Disco Elysium*. His claim to be the best cook in the band, with pizza sandwiches being a speciality, may be disputed! **Kyle** and **Woody** have produced DJ sets together at student unions around the country.

Dan Smith, an inadvertent polymath, created the band in 2010 and is the songwriter and lead singer. A reluctant violin player at school, now he will play piano and keyboards, drums and guitar, and has a vocal range of three octaves. A London marathon runner and the most energetic member of the band, covering the entire stage at almost every show. He will also jump into the crowd, sometimes with hapless results and other times much happier. Dan also co-produces the records and has co-directed one of their music videos. He could also be known as 'Upper-Case Man'.

Songs for, and with, other singers are written and recorded as well as music for documentary films and iconic TV programmes. He has also sung for a Christmas advert. Other interests have led to him being a judge for book awards and for unsigned artist competitions, co-presenting a podcast series about books and libraries with book reviews and author interviews. He has appeared on a TV book review programme. I have read several of the books Dan has recommended and enjoyed about half of them! Sadly my taste is lightweight.

He is the band member that invariably answers the questions from interviewers and will reply at length and comprehensively! The questions are often turned around by asking the reporters how *they* are or what *they* think and when he says 'good question' you know he is stalling and trying to think of an answer. ☺ Dan has a unique interpretation of the word **SOON**, which can mean any time between tomorrow and next year, which totally exasperates the fans. He is undoubtedly a softie, always willing to cuddle puppies, chickens, goats, snakes and koalas, to name but a few.

Each member of the band supports other, often unsigned musicians by helping with writing, producing or playing. Two singers from gospel choirs often accompany the band, **Bimbola Adebiyi,** known as Bim, and **Senab Adekunle,** and their voices enrich the band's sound.

I discovered Bastille very late in their journey, during Glastonbury 2019. I was planning to watch all the acts on BBC iPlayer. I got to B for Bastille and did not move any further! The upbeat tempo, the variety of songs and Dan's accent were all part of the attraction! I was bowled over by the sad lyrics about world events as well as everyday struggles that were often given catchy dance-along music. Unusually for me, because Dan's enunciation was so clear, I actually listened to his lyrics and for the most part understood what he meant. Although even now I still smile when I 'mishear' the word octopus instead of optimist! There are bands around whose lyrics are incomprehensible to me!

Bastille are repeatedly described as one of the friendliest, most generous bands in the business by other groups, singers, the crew, the media and by their fans and aunties! They never appear to argue, nor do they publicly complain about each other. I would add that they are extremely talented, charitable and Dan is kind to old ladies, as you will see next. It was a happy day for me when I chose to follow such an exceptional group of musicians. Many of the qualities mentioned above, particularly friendliness, also apply to almost all of the fans I have met, experiencing many kind moments from all nationalities that follow Bastille.

3. A trip to the royal palace

 A combination of bad decisions led me to think a big festival was going to be right for me, so to give myself a greater chance of being closer to the stage and seeing a longer performance, I resolved to search for concerts in smaller venues in future. Therefore, tickets for a show at Hampton Court Palace, Henry VIII's home, near London, were bought.

This time my son **Mark** came with me. With permission to park in the palace grounds we were surprised to see members of the band were also parking there.

I was astonished when my favourite singer, Dan, came across and chatted to me. He was very kind and we talked about the joy of being allowed out again after lockdown, about the magnificent palace and the story of my t-shirt emblazoned with their name. He asked where we would be sitting and said he would see us later. He then gave me a big hug, which was the first I had received since Covid began!

Mark and I made our way around the palace and into the beautiful gardens, where we met other fans of the band, including **Pauline,** who had followed the band since the days they played in pubs. The time came to go inside to the courtyard where the show was going to take place. It was then that I discovered how bumpy it is to ride in a wheelchair over cobblestones. Hampton Court is 500 years old and so are the paths inside. I had to hold on to my hat and I wished I had brought a cushion. ☺ I blame the Tudor builders!

The band came on stage and played newly re-orchestrated versions of my favourite songs, complete with a large orchestra and choir. It was a fantastic addition to their list of accomplishments. Rick Astley was a surprise guest. Later, without warning, Dan jumped off the stage and into the audience while he was still singing 'Of the Night'.

Some of the girls squealed and giggled when he came near them, giving out high fives and handshakes, but he carried on, skipping towards the wheelchair platform, and all of a sudden there he was, asking me for another hug!

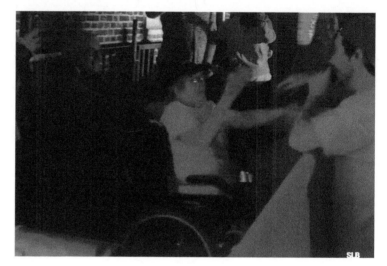

Give me a hug!

High-fiving along the cobbles

All the way home that night I had a silly smile on my face from amazement. ☺ It was the first time I had ever met anyone remotely famous, let alone be hugged by one, twice!

Arriving home well past my bedtime at quarter past midnight, an idea that it would be an excellent adventure to follow this friendly band around the country was triggered. Lists of family and friends who might like to join me were noted and the next day plans were made and tickets bought.

<u>Buying tickets for disabled customers</u>

As I am always on wheels for concerts and events, a friend is allowed a free ticket in order to help me through the crowds, to make sure I am safely removed if there is a fire (and to buy the drinks). Finding someone to be my 'carer' is normally straightforward.

1. Invite carer, preferably one who likes the band.
2. Research the venue and the facilities for the disabled.
   One venue said, 'We welcome disabled visitors and by the way there are eighteen steps down to the performance area!'
3. Send proof of disability. Every venue requires this before tickets are issued.
   Invariably each site/promoter has different requirements and provisions, favourites involve a call or email to a real person. I try to organise this before buying tickets.
   Those bought from the venue are rarely eligible for pre-sale codes.
   I do have an ACCESS card, purchased as a device to be excused from sending proof every time, but it only seems to cover London venues at the moment.
4. Ensure a ticket for my carer is recorded. Sometimes this is an extra e-ticket, other times we just have to turn up!
5. Book my place and a seat for my carer on the wheelchair platform if there is one.
   Try to find out where it is in relation to the stage.
6. Research the car parking and book if possible/necessary.
7. Research and book an accessible hotel near the venue if we are too far from home.

Once I was in a queue online with over 70,000 people trying to buy tickets when there should have been a separate queue for the considerably smaller number of disabled seats. The 90-minute wait proved unsuccessful. It would be quite easy to admit defeat, but since retirement time is not usually an issue. ☹ I believe the procedure is an altogether more complicated task for disabled buyers and could be simplified. A few venues/ promoters are making some progress. GoogleMaps are invaluable for # 2, 6 and 7.

I should also say that most venues treat disabled customers well and with kindness. On arrival we are normally allowed to get to the front of any queues so that we can find our place before the rest of audience pours in.

4. Up close and personal

During lockdown I was asked to join a Facebook group called 'All This Bad Blood Here' set up by **Lana** for Bastille fans. During a Zoom meeting a group of us chatted and later in my story I actually met two of the group, namely **Rita** in Southampton and **Kim** from Cornwall. Getting to know fans not only in the UK but also Europe, such as **Olivia** in France and **Cori** in America, via posts and comments has been very interesting.

THE BROOK

The next show was at a small grassroots venue in Southampton, the Brook. My young neighbour **Georgina** and I met **Rita**, my new online friend, on the way. We were allowed in first with the wheelchair, so we took the space in the middle at the very front. Everyone was standing except me, until the end that is. This was a mini-tour and that night only Dan, Charlie and Will were playing. The stage was small so perhaps the whole band would not have fit.

There was a minor incident before the show started, a girl decided she would lean on my wheelchair so that I couldn't put my arm on the armrest. I gently elbowed her and she moved away only to come back even closer. My reaction was to nudge her firmly, which upset her so much that she loudly said, 'You're pushing me!' Too right I was, but she was almost sitting on me. My two companions and several other fans began to remonstrate with her over her treatment of the disabled fan. Her reply was 'What are you doing here anyway?' Boom. All the girls around me, in chorus, told her to 'Go away', but less politely than that! She did as she was told.

When Dan came out, he spotted me and mouthed, 'Hi, you al right?' with a big smile. He had not seen me for five months! Of course, Dan may say that to all old ladies but I'm happy to believe that the grey hair, the wheelchair and being much older than everyone else had jogged his memory! My new defenders then wondered who I was!

It was one of those nights, especially intimate and everyone determined to have a good time. In fact, when Dan took off his jacket someone wolf-whistled and it made him laugh so much that he couldn't start the next song. Charlie made a start but didn't help when he sang "Get drunk, take your coat off!" which set Dan giggling again. A most unusual version of 'Good Grief'!

The venue was so compact that we were almost leaning on the speakers and when Charlie started playing 'Power' the sound was so deep and loud that my drink, resting on the top, danced along to the vibes, luckily nothing was spilled.

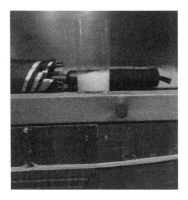

5. Off to the seaside

We had so much fun that Rita and I decided to see the band together a few months later, in Bournemouth, the lovely seaside town in Dorset. Rita enjoyed seeing the long sandy beaches that reminded her of her home country of Malaysia. The band played new songs from their brand-new album, *Give Me the Future*, this was the first show of the tour. Quite a lot the fans already knew the words and sang along, which made Dan smile. The futuristic set included 'trip-hazard' light bars scattered all over the stage. The audience experienced a journey in and out of the 'Innerverse', a virtual world with great on-screen effects.

Luckily, the band all managed to avoid the hazards! Later when they sang 'Pompeii', their first hit, I stood up and held onto the barrier around the platform to join in the dancing (although I only swayed and waved my arm a bit!). 😉

The band then toured all around the country playing their new music. I asked another friend, **Daniela**, if she would like to see them in Plymouth, another city beside the sea. She agreed and on Easter Sunday we travelled to the West Country and arrived at our hotel, only to find the entrance had several steps up to it. That was a test for me! We were later allowed to use a side door that had a ramp, the tradesman's entrance!

We went to a Q&A session before the show and I gave Dan a t-shirt with a drawing of him on it made by a clever artist, **Ian Young** of Skwiggles Co., which was created at my request.

While queueing we met **Anne** (with an E), a friend of Rita's, who had come from Germany and was following the band all around the UK.

Later Daniela and I were outside the hotel waiting for our special door to be opened when who should come along? It was Dan with his friends. We had a little chat and he thanked me for the t-shirt and gave me my third hug!

Plymouth is the city where Woody grew up, so a lot of his friends were in the audience. The supporting band, **The Native**, are also from Plymouth. They were happy to play in their hometown, especially when they got such a loud reception. I had previously sent a message to them on social media saying it was going to be a riot in Plymouth and they replied that it would be 'Carnage'! And it sounded like it was from where I was sitting! Dan revealed that Bastille had been taken to a 'lively' nightclub by The Native the night before and that some of the party were still recovering!

Previously, during the interval, we heard someone behind us shout 'Oi, Mo', and I looked up and saw my online friend **Kim** hanging over the balcony and waving at me. Kim had said she would be there because she lived nearby. Everyone around laughed at us happily shouting and waving at each other!

As we left the theatre the path was a bit steep and Daniela was finding it difficult to push the wheelchair up, but two lovely people, who were very happy and giggly (!), decided they would help and grabbed hold of it and raced up the slope at great speed. I was holding on for dear life, laughing along with them and leaving poor Daniela behind! Later, in the hotel, we met two fans who had come all the way from America, **Kimberley** and her friend **Kristin**, as well as two more from Italy, **Giulia** and **Faustine**, and then Kim and her boyfriend **William** joined us too. It was the first time Kim and I had actually met face to face! More hugs! We had a great time sharing stories and we all still send messages to each other online. Of course, they were treated to the photos of me chatting to Dan! The only reason that this group of former strangers were together having fun was because we all liked Bastille, it was an extra bonus for me! I thought all my new friends were lovely.

6. We must go down to the sea again

John and I had a holiday during the summer while Bastille went to America and Europe playing music in many cities. When they returned to England, they decided to play at the Victorious festival on Southsea Common, next to the sea again. My resolve to go to smaller venues didn't last long!

This time I travelled with **Aaron**, my neighbour, and met up with Rita again. Before the music started all of the band were in a record store signing copies of the new album. Aaron, Rita and I joined the queue and had photos taken too.

Kyle, Dan, Will and Woody with Mo

While in the queue a girl with pink hair came and hugged me tightly and tearfully said I was a legend and the queen of Bastille fans! I had no idea who she was but she had read my FB posts about my experiences seeing the band. I expect I was 'queen' because of my age! I was very surprised and Rita and Aaron (and others) were chuckling at my embarrassment and kept calling me 'Your Majesty!'

It was a long day and eventually the battery on the scooter lost power, which forced the decision to see **Paolo Nutini**, who was playing at the same time as **Bastille**, but Paolo's stage was nearer the car park! Rita went to see the boys. There are no brakes on a mobility scooter, you just have to stop accelerating, but amazingly not one of the hundreds of fans leaving the venue with us was run over as Aaron pushed me to the car park. The scooter does have a horn to warn people when I am behind them, but it sounds more like a little bird in a nest, cheep cheep, not a good loud BEEP! ☺

Just before Christmas I bought tickets to see Bastille and other bands in Lancaster the following year (2023) for the Highest Point Festival. It would be six months to wait, so Rita decided that my horizons should be broadened and we should see some other bands. We saw the **Amazons** and **Deaf Havana** in Southampton and **Joywave** in London and had three memorable nights out.

Daniel from Joywave who 'illicitly' marketed my Bastille t-shirt

Rita proved to be a most enthusiastic 'carer'; not only is she mad keen on Bastille, she was lucky enough to attend the MTV Unplugged show, but she also goes to many different concerts and gigs every year. She always pays her way and even gives me half the ticket price yet hers, as carer, are free. We have remarkably similar tastes, even though she is much younger than me. She is very friendly, chatting to security guards, other fans, band crews, and of course the band.

7. When we discover that it's not grim up north at all

The time came to travel 270 miles to Lancaster. It took us a while, but we arrived at our hotel despite the satnav telling me I would find it in the middle of a dual carriageway. Next morning we had a buffet breakfast in the hotel with Kate and her family who live in Lancaster, and some toast and fruit found its way into a napkin for my lunch! Rita and I decided to visit Lancaster Castle, because we were keen on the history, it being a former prison, much like the Bastille in Paris but without the storming or the revolution.

We made our way to the front gate of the castle feeling every one of the cobblestones, again. The path to the gate was fairly steep and had a peculiar arch and bend in it. It was at this point that Rita **saved my life**. My 'untippable' scooter, the *Titanic* of the mobility world, started to tip over, falling towards the ground. Rita's superpowers kicked in and she managed to shove both me and the scooter back onto four wheels. I was saved and able to continue without any further frights. It would have been a very messy heap of bodies if Rita had not been so quick and we would have certainly missed Bastille. She is my heroine and she made sure I did not run into trouble again.

Lancaster Castle main gate

All the staff at the Highest Point Festival venue, Williamson Park, were friendly, funny and helpful. The park is paved but very hilly and we were worried that the scooter wouldn't last the night, so we found the disabled platform and parked up, in pole position with a good view of the stage!

We both like to arrive early. Only *six* hours to wait but there was plenty of entertainment on the stage and amongst the crowd. We are always easy to find at a venue, upon the platform, usually in an elevated position. Several fan friends came over, including **Tiff**, who is American, **Alessia** from Italy and **Rebecca and James** from Preston! Rebecca had seen my FB message that we would be there and where we would be and she sent me a picture of what she would be wearing so that I could spot her! On the platform Rita quickly made friends with **Zoe,** from Manchester, who was sitting beside her with her mum, and they were going to every show.

We were enjoying **Freya Ridings** on the stage when Rita loudly whispered, 'There's Dan!' and pointed to the crowd in the front. She asked whether she should run and tell him that I was there. I laughingly replied, 'Yes', but was surprised when she jumped up and ran all the way over to him. She said, 'Mo's here, come and see her!' to which he apparently said, 'No way!' and promptly made his way over! Both of us speaking rhetorically! I couldn't believe what Rita had done but looked up and saw that Dan coming towards us on the platform. He had a bit of trouble with the platform security but suddenly he was there giving me a huge, long hug.

He was surprised to see me standing, on most other occasions I have been sitting on wheels. He probably didn't notice my white knuckles gripping the fence for balance! He asked me how I was, twice, and said it was great to see me and I mostly burbled replies! He willingly signed Rita's birthday card for the next day, then he took a selfie of us on *his* phone! I am fairly sure he lies in bed at night and dreams of me! Haha. 😊😣

Then Rita asked him to write a few lines of her favourite lyrics on a piece of card and to sign a drumstick from their show at Lord's Cricket Ground.

I was given another hug and Dan left, slowly because everyone else wanted him to sign things! He just showed how full of warmth he was and how truly kind and patient he was with all his adoring fans, whatever their age.

James took a lot of photos of all this and he and Rebecca were in the right place to get their own picture with Dan. Zoe was also busy with her phone, taking photos too.

Dan, James and Rebecca

22

Just after he left Kate arrived with her partner **David** and my granddaughter **Mia**. They demanded proof that Dan had visited us and that they had just missed him! The photos did the trick.

This performance was a warm-up for the *Bad Blood* ten-year anniversary tour, BBX, later in the year. When the band came on stage they gave a great show, everyone enjoying the older songs once more. When Dan was speaking to me earlier, he said he was extremely nervous about singing the old songs again as it had been a long time since they had played some of them! I told him they would be fine and they were. ☺ Amazing in fact. The songs were played in the order of the album, so they started with 'Pompeii', which seemed very odd as it is normally the finale.

Nervous Dan....

Before we left, at the end of the show, Woody threw his drumsticks into the crowd and our new friend James caught one. He very kindly presented it to Rita, who is the collector amongst us! She was taken aback by his kindness.

The scooter just about made it up and down the hills of the park and back to the car. Phew. Everyone leaving sounded as though they had really enjoyed themselves by singing the chorus of 'Pompeii' as they strode along. Eh Eh Oh Eh Oh. It was a very relaxed and good-humoured event. And at least two of us, possibly three, had the best time ever!

Next day, at breakfast, Rita read her birthday card several times, reading Dan's words! She was very pleased with it and said she would have to buy a frame!

8. Summer nights

Two months later Rita and I made our way to the Royal Botanic Gardens at Kew, west London, to see Bastille, again. Just before this we squeezed in a **Hozier** concert in Bournemouth, which was excellent apart from the lousy view we had, at floor level behind a standing audience.

We arrived in Kew early at about 3.30pm and when I tried to gain the attention of a young member of staff things got a bit scary. In my excitement I drove my scooter towards her and totally forgot that the 'brake' I was using was, in fact, the accelerator! Whoosh I went, with people scattering everywhere! I eventually came to my senses, let go of everything and ground to a halt, leaving Rita to pick up any bodies!

The arrangements were that the security gates would be open at 5pm when the queueing fans would be allowed in for bag checks and the 'doors' would be open at 6pm. The girl got her breath back and then explained that at this time we had to pay £20 each to enter the gardens and then leave and queue outside with the fans at 5pm. Maybe the girl still felt vulnerable near my scooter, or perhaps she sensed our urgent need for the toilet, but she relented and said we could enter, free of charge, use the loo and then exit by another place, well away from her, such as the Elizabeth Gate on the far side of the gardens to join the queue there. Excellent. The accessible toilet was not very wide so I had to reverse into it, and for this performance we could have sold tickets, in, out, forwards, backwards, regular hokey-cokey. Mission eventually accomplished and no further casualties, just a few near misses. I really need a rear-view mirror!

The glory of the gardens was exceptional, with beautiful flowers and trees from all over the world. We slowly made our way to the Elizabeth Gate, enjoying the fabulous displays. We waited inside for things to begin. Eventually we took our place on the w'chair platform and had a good view of the stage and of the people sitting on blankets with their posh Fortnum & Mason picnic hampers. Rita and I took our own sandwiches and cold chicken!

Before the music started quite a few fan friends came to say hello. Zoe, who was at Lancaster, came and chatted and meanwhile, at the barrier, her mum was talking to **Paula,** who I first met at Hampton Court Palace. She made her way over as well. We had stayed in touch and enjoyed having a long catch-up. Several others came by, one gave us bracelets with Bastille decorations on, and we all promised to meet up at other gigs. I was delighted that the young fans were happy to include me in their gang.

The band played their best songs and Dan went into the crowd twice. This turns out to be a regular occurrence, but he did not come over to our platform. So, Rita and I had several hugs from friends but none from Dan! The exit from the gardens was almost as eventful as my entry. Half of the audience left through a single gateway and it was a bit of a squash. Being at a low level people do not realise the scooter is there until they step into my path and get a reminder on their ankles. We learned a good lesson there and vowed to leave later next time.

9. Last but not least

The final Bastille 2023 concert that Rita and I were going to together took place at Warwick Castle. It involved an overnight stay but with a new battery in the scooter, we sped along from the hotel to the castle. Once again we made new friends and met old ones too. Rita's friend Tiff gave us each another

bracelet and **Liz** came for a long chat, **Sarah** and **Lorraine** both came to say hello. I had met all three before at Hampton Court and the Brook. Zoe and her mum were there as well as other fan friends of Rita, including **Char** from Germany. It's always a relief to discover that we are not the only fans travelling far and wide to see their favourite band.

Warwick was where the disabled tickets came into their own. We were directed immediately inside, leaving behind a long queue of other fans snaking around the castle walls. We were given entry bracelets and directions and after our tickets were checked we were in. No embarrassing moments with the staff this time. In fact, every one of the staff members was courteous and there was a happy atmosphere all round, all night.

On our way into the courtyard we saw **Dick Meredith**, the band's tour manager, with a colleague walking towards us. Rita said, 'Hi Dick', and he seemed to recognise us and smiled and asked us how we were doing. Dick can be seen in lots of photos of Dan, usually when holding his hand when Dan chooses to leap up on the barrier to join the crowd.

We were directed to the disabled platform and the lady in charge, **Alicia,** told us we could sit where we liked. Rita chose pole position (again) which was next to the sound tent. We were facing the very centre of the stage, which was not too far away.

Rita and Mo in pole position again, first on the platform

Warwick Castle: In this pic right the sound tent is the grey square with the ramp up to the platform behind it and you can determine where we were if you see, above, the white-roofed toilets behind us and then again here.

While we were waiting, I went to the merch stand to buy a t-shirt for **Cori**, my American friend. There was quite a queue for the goods, but we all had a laugh when I asked for the same t-shirt that I was wearing and the lad looked around and said, 'I'm sorry, we don't seem to have any of those.' We all cracked up because at his feet there was a crate chock full of them!

> ### Merchandise
>
> *Bastille fans will be all too familiar with the merchandise sold as souvenirs of the band, usually t-shirts, hoodies, caps, posters and knick-knacks. I am reassured by the fact that I am not alone in buying almost every new design t-shirt, which regularly appear with each new album and tour and not forgetting various products for charity. I am probably the only one who thinks I am single-handedly keeping the wolf from the band's door by purchasing the merch! Of course the CDs and vinyls have to be bought too. And I am still waiting to find out what we can do with our **Survivin'** coins!*
>
> *Alternatively, some devotees are highly creative and make their own personal items, usually including the ubiquitous triangle logo which also takes a new form every new tour. The triangle appears on bracelets, earrings, necklaces and even tattoos as testament to their allegiance. Perhaps they are exhibited for the benefit of their fan friends as much as for the band's amusement. Some of the fans are particularly artistic, with beautiful drawings and paintings and even crocheted dolls representing the band members!*

It was time to open our smuggled picnic (no food or drink allowed here!). Our handbags and backpacks had been searched but the bag on the back of the scooter was untouched! Rita made friends with the two women behind us and I embarrassingly flaunted my collection of photos of me meeting Dan and happened to mention the number of hugs! (5) If you can't show off amongst Bastille fans, where can you? They were very sweet and approved of my pictures! Rita found out that they were mother and daughter and mother was not that much of a fan, but she may have changed her mind later!

After three warm-up acts Bastille arrived. When 'Overjoyed' was played Woody was front of stage ready with his electronic drums. I noticed two tech guys running to the back of the stage and also some smoke. Fearing the worst, the smoke turned out to be special effects and Woody then pointed out that his drums were not working. He gave up eventually, despite the efforts of the crew, and returned to his fail-safe acoustic drum kit! Amid all this excitement the band continued splendidly with the song!

We could see the whole stage and knew that Dan was going to do a walkabout in the crowd when he put on his 'anti-grope' jacket. He strode off the stage, over the barrier, made his way through the crowd, with Dick in tow on bodyguard duty. He came towards the disabled platform at the back while singing 'Flaws'. They then came up the ramp and Dan advanced along all the wheelchairs and crutches, fist-bumping and tapping everyone, still singing over the fence to the audience below. He got to our end and to my astonishment reached me and planted a kiss on my cheek. I didn't even know he had seen us! I had to sit down after that!

Mwah!

A video of it ended up on YouTube and you can hear the crowd around me going 'Aaah' when I got my kiss. Even Dick applauded. I usually put a couple of pictures on Facebook and am pleased to receive comments and wise cracks from the fan groups, my family and friends. Everyone was sweet with their comments although 'restraining orders' and 'stalking' came up quite often from my family, along with nursing home ideas! So much for family ties!

My old school friends think I am irredeemable! But I think that's envy! I have never once said that I would grow old with grace! ☺ It was a wonderful day spent with a lovely group of fans in an excellent venue. And it was sealed with a kiss. ✖

I love the attention (of course) but I am mystified. Rita and I are casual fans compared with some we know who go to every show, some travelling all over the UK and Europe, and further afield for gigs. But on this occasion, it was me that got a kiss! I think it might be because I am recognisable, safe, not likely to scream or try to rip his clothes off, etc.! I'm the same age as his mother after all. Who knows? I think the answer is that he is humble, perfectly grounded, kind-hearted and considerate to his fans.

This adventure took place over two years, and I believe that there were no bad days when I was with my wheels, friends and music. I am incredibly grateful to all my 'carers' for their kind attention and the laughs we had, from the winking, smiling, unknown man over breakfast in Plymouth that set Daniela and I giggling, to being named 'queen' of fans in Southsea and Rita putting me straight at Lancaster Castle. It has shown me that even with seemingly insurmountable mobility issues and advancing age, with some careful application and intent and the support of thoughtful companions and venue staff, pretty much anything is possible. It has been a proper experience which had not been imagined when I first tuned into Glastonbury in 2019. Without doubt there are not enough words to thank Dan Smith for his part in the story. Thank you, Dan.

December 2023

ANSWERS: No Bad Days, *but if you close your eyes*, World Gone Mad, Dancing in the Dark, Happier, Bad Decisions, Joy, Blame, Of the Night, Quarter Past Midnight, Admit Defeat, Those Nights, Good Grief, Power, Give Me the Future, Pompeii, *holding on for dear life*, Falling, Run into Trouble, Dreams, Warmth, Bad Blood, Overjoyed, *eh eh oh eh oh*, Free, Another Place, Glory, Good Lesson, Flaws, Family Ties, *grow old with grace*.

CREDITS AND ACKNOWLEDGEMENTS

Bodyguards:

Mark Aspinwall
Kate Aspinwall
David Reid
William Aspinwall
Mia Aspinwall
Georgina Halsall
Rita Jokiaho
Daniela Olaru
Aaron Halsall

Staff at:

Latitude Festival, Suffolk
Hampton Court Palace
The Brook, Southampton
Bournemouth BIC
Plymouth Pavilions
Victorious Festival, Southsea
Pie & Vinyl Record Store
Highest Point Festival, Lancaster
Royal Botanic Gardens, Kew
Warwick Castle

Proofreaders & Advisers:

Kerry Aspinwall
Kate Aspinwall
Lana Harvey
Cori Knox
Ian Young
Susan Smith
'Louise Sawyer' /Rita J
Wayne Richardson

PHOTO CREDITS

Most of the photos are my own but I have permission to use others from
Rita, Alessia, James, Zoe, Char, Daniela, Sarah, Georgina, Mark, Kate.
~~~~~~

Special thanks go to my long-suffering husband, John, who 'enjoys' plenty of Bastille music at home and in my car, to Rita Jokiaho for being an excellent companion and to Ian and Diane Young for their encouragement.

Links
https://skwiggles.co.uk/
https://chooselove.org/

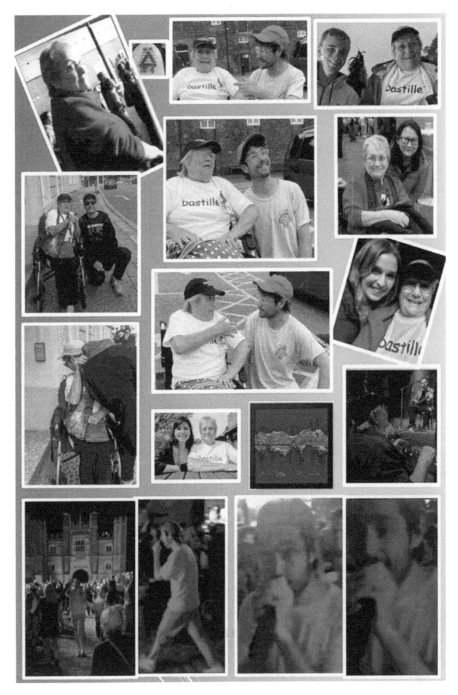